CHANGE YOUR POSTURE! CHANGE YOUR *Life!*

Affirmation Journal
Volume 11 — Kindness

D Nicole Williams

Sh'Shares NETWORK
www.ShShares.com

CHANGE YOUR POSTURE! CHANGE YOUR LIFE!
AFFIRMATION JOURNAL

Volume 11 — Kindness

For permission requests, write to the publisher, addressed
"ATTN: Permissions" at the following:

Sh'Shares NETWORK, LLC
1601-1 N Main Street 13202
Jacksonville, FL 32206-0202
www.ShShares.com

Bulk discounts are available on quantity purchases by associations, corporations, and others for business, educational and ministry use. For details, contact the publisher at the address above.

Library of Congress Control Number: 2016918044

ISBN: 978-1-942650-37-9

VOL. 01: 978-1-942650-27-0 (Journal, Faithfulness)
VOL. 02: 978-1-942650-28-7 (Journal, Joy)
VOL. 03: 978-1-942650-29-4 (Journal, Peace)
VOL. 04: 978-1-942650-30-0 (Journal, Wisdom)
VOL. 05: 978-1-942650-31-7 (Journal, Diligence)
VOL. 06: 978-1-942650-32-4 (Journal, Self-Control)
VOL. 07: 978-1-942650-33-1 (Journal, Goodness)
VOL. 08: 978-1-942650-34-8 (Journal, Patience)
VOL. 09: 978-1-942650-35-5 (Journal, Gentleness)
VOL. 10: 978-1-942650-36-2 (Journal, Humility)
VOL. 12: 978-1-942650-38-6 (Journal, Love)

Printed in the United States of America
FIRST EDITION

Kindness

Posture 03. Passion for OTHERS

11. Kindness

introduction

Greetings Posture Changer!

I am very pleased that you have opted to join me on this journey to Change Your Posture! Change Your LIFE! I am excited for what the future holds in store for you, and I am looking forward to each of your triumphs as they will undoubtedly help you arrive at your predestined seat of GREATNESS! As each of us treks along, we must be reminded to be conscious of others and their connection to our own purpose. The more that we can pay it forward to others, the more we amass exceeding benefits in return. Remembering this, employ increased levels of kindness and watch your life be blessed in return.

As you journey, please take the time to share your progress. Email me at SHINE@change-your-posture.com! I'd LOVE to hear your hopes, helps, and hiccups along the way!!!

I anticipate that you'll build your personal connections and have GREAT progress despite these—sometimes heavy—processes, so don't forget to keep me posted! ttyl

With Thoughts of Kindness,
— Coach D!

How to Get the MOST Out of This Journal…

- **Read. Write. Reflect.**
- **Cry …***if you need to…*
- **Phone a friend and let's get major WORK done in our lives with these journals!!!**

Take the time that you need to be the friend YOU need. Do it for YOU! Don't wait for another! This is the season to take over your life and take control of your thoughts through affirmation!

- **Thought bubbles are included throughout the journal so you can share your own thoughts and reflections.**
- **There are boxes included for you to doodle OR maybe you use them as spaces to ask questions of yourself… that's up to you!**

No matter what you use each space for, be sure that you are authentic! This is *your* time and this is *your* space to be the YOU that YOU need for YOU! Do it now. Show YOURSELF what YOU are made of…

Change Your Posture! Change Your LIFE!

Kindness

01 Kindness

"

I Will Work on KINDNESS!

"

Kindness is an expression of goodness toward others. It's a showing of high regard for people you come in contact with.

Kindness Affirmation *(Repeat this aloud)*

To be kind is to act for the good of other people at all times. Through kindness and respect, I show myself useful and fit. I adapt myself in servitude and sweetness, exhibiting compassion and sympathy with no sign of abrasiveness.

To the beautiful people who cross your path, may you fill their days with many, many hugs and kisses, much fun, laughter and boatloads of AWESOMENESS! Words alone can't always sufficiently express how much people mean to you, but you can let them know you're thankful through random acts of kindness.

This month is focused on kindness and your displays of gentleness and tenderheartedness toward others. We review methods of kindness which enable you to go even further in your aim to be a model of kindness.

Say Aloud: **I Will Work on Kindness! I Will Be Kind!**

Journal Prompt...

What does kindness mean to me?

____

____

____

How can I work on kindness within my life?

____

____

____

____

Prayer of Kindness

Compose a dedicated *Prayer of Kindness* that you will work on this month.

Consider the areas of life where you would like to see kindness. If you get stuck, discuss the concept of kindness with your coach, an accountability partner or a friend.

Fill this entire page with your kindness prayer.

Print it. Post it. Read it daily.

02 Kindness

“

I Will CHANGE My ATTITUDE!

”

Face it: life can be tough!!! You face so many battles and so many circumstances that can break you down if you encounter them with the wrong attitude. As you grow and evolve, so too do your attitudes. Attitudes are a reflection of your experiences. They show progressive evolution toward a more positive direction.

It's always said that if you want something you've never had, you must do things you've never done. As you drift away from former friends as you *grow* your separate ways, you should also be drifting FAR away from your former SELF! With everything around you constantly changing, how can you possibly stay the same?

Say Aloud: **I Will Change My Attitude! I Will Change My Life!**

A renewed attitude comes with renewed focus, a renewed mentality and abundance of new hope! Life looks MUCH brighter once the viewing lens is changed.

Your attitude is like a box of crayons that color your world.
Constantly color your picture gray, and your picture will always be bleak.
Try adding some bright colors to the picture by including humor,
and your picture begins to lighten up.

ALLEN KLEIN

Attitude Adjustment

Which elements of my attitude do I need to adjust NOW?

1. Using the chart below, jot down 10 attitude adjustments that you need to MAKE!
2. Create a deadline for making adjustments and find yourself some accountability partners!!!
3. At the point of completion, check off each adjustment as you drop poor attitudes one by one!

10 Attitude Adjustments I Need to Make	Deadline	✓

Who Will I Connect with for Accountability?
My Coach
My Accountability Partner
My Friend

Kindness

“

I Will LISTEN to Others!

”

Within the world, there exists the illogical idea that a person’s status, position, role or *lack* of status, position or role removes their right to an opinion. Au contraire! The fact that a person does *not* hold a certain role MANDATES their right to an opinion! Why? This is a DEMOCRACY!!! Opinions are STANDARD! Your very own LIFE is a democracy being that it is SO governed by the popular opinion—albeit the popular opinion may rightfully be your *own*!!! ☺

Don’t readily dismiss the input of other individuals. Considering the fact that a person cares enough about you to even *share* their input shows their concern, their thought and their simple acknowledgment of your presence within their lives. *You should be grateful!* The people who care the MOST are likely identical to the ones who *talk* the most. Learn to listen! As freely as you volunteer and impart your own ”wisdom” to others, be as apt to hear what others have to say to you in return! Admittedly, all of the feedback that you receive may not be applicable—that’s perfectly fine within this context! Today’s affirmation is about the basis of *listening* more than proper application technique!

Make a practice of listening to understand versus merely listening to respond.

Say Aloud: **I Will Listen to Others! I Will Listen to Understand!**

Kindness

“

I Will Be PEACEFUL!

”

Peace in your life is a concept that you must be proactive about. You can't sit around and *wait* for peace to find you! You have to CREATE peace in *every* moment and *every* second of *every* day!

Being peaceful means coming from a place of balance and wholeness. It means existing in a framework where all is well *within* you no matter what is happening *around* you. Since you can't control your outside environment, you must constantly arm yourself with the ability to stay calm on the *inside*.

Peace is your safety net. Peace is your sanity when all else has gone COMPLETELY insane. Prioritize peace in life. Without it, you will soon find that the rest of life's luxuries amount to little without peace as their constant companion.

Be peaceful! No matter what life brings your way, commit yourself to peaceful resolve.

Say Aloud: **I Will Be Peaceful!**

Circumstances are beyond human control,
but our conduct is in our own power.

Benjamin Disraeli

Journal Prompt...

Am I being peaceful in my life? _ _ _ _ _ _ **How so?** _ _ _ _ _ _ _ _ _ _ _ _ _ _

How can I work to create a more peaceful life?

05 Kindness

"I Will Be a Better FRIEND!"

Being a better friend means learning to listen when your friends aren't audibly speaking. It means learning to see what isn't readily obvious. It means being more for them than you'd have them to be for you. The BEST friends are those who are selfless—those who don't allow limitations of the title to keep them from showing brotherly or sisterly love to all who are accepted as kindred spirits. Operation within the role of *friend* is a privilege that should never be taken lightly.

Friendship is a great honor to bestow and behold. Friends are the sisters and brothers that you get to choose. Readily embrace them as such by happily welcoming friends into your world.

Appreciation for friendship is best shown by returning the favor. People sometimes make the mistake of letting misunderstandings, distance or other insignificant factors interfere with the progression of friendships. Great friends are one of the most valued treasures on earth, so it is in your best interest to forgive and forget all wrongdoings in situations that are worthy of continuation. Friends add so much value to your life that *letting go* shouldn't always be as easy as you make it. The same goes for you—*walking away* from friends shouldn't be an easy thing to do. Sometimes, you just need to tough it out. In some friendships, you need to commit as a sister or a brother rather than just as a friend.

Journal Prompt...

What elements are missing from my friendships?

How can I be a better friend?

06 Kindness

"

I Will Let My Light SHINE!

"

My personal meditation, prayer and relaxation practices often involve candles. For me, candles represent peace, reverence and adoration. Candles are a representation of shine, brilliance and light. During any of the aforementioned processes, I am reminded to let my light shine, and no matter what I am *growing* through, this reminder brings me peace.

I recommend this process for *anyone* struggling with *anything*. Just light a candle. No need to watch it. Go about your day and *see* GOD move!!!

Candles are regularly lit at various times for various reasons. Going forward, light candles for yourself remembering that you've been given something to share with others. Your light is a gift to the world. It should be shared at all times possible—even when you don't feel like it! Whenever you can, **SHINE YOUR LIGHT!**

Know that YOU are a gift to the world. YOU are in GOD's hands. Be a ready representation of God's grace by letting your light so shine!

Say Aloud: **I Will Let My Light Shine! I Embody God's Grace!**

Keep your face to the sunshine and you cannot see a shadow.

HELEN KELLER

Journal Prompt...

In what new ways will I Let My Light Shine?

1. ______________________________
2. ______________________________
3. ______________________________
4. ______________________________
5. ______________________________
6. ______________________________
7. ______________________________
8. ______________________________

07 Kindness

"I Will RESPECT My Partner!"

Too many relationships come together without respect. People exist within fiery frameworks where there is no mutual honor, loyalty or high regard for the other party involved. This is **COMPLETELY** unacceptable! Of all that you owe any other human being—especially those with whom you've chosen to share your lives—respect is MOST vital. A standard of respect creates the foundation for all other positive attributes to be appropriately developed and sustained.

Your engagements are a direct reflection of how you view yourself. If you decide to withhold honor, loyalty and respect from yourself, be responsible enough not to involve the unsuspecting in your own damaging exploits.

Respecting your partner means exhibiting timeless love and honor that is free from limitations. The decisions you make regarding them shouldn't feel like sacrifices. You should be more than happy to take EVERY opportunity to ensure your partner knows that you appreciate them and their love.

Affirmation Journal

★ **In what areas am I lacking respect from my partner?**

★ **In what areas am I lacking respect for my partner?**

★ **In what ways can I show more respect for my partner?**

★ **How can I implement necessary changes?**

Kindness

"

I Will SMILE!

"

Smiles are blessings. Laughter is a gift. Why not share the JOY of those pleasantries with others? Each time that you do, you are not only blessing others by sharing your gift but you are also honoring God. You reap what you sow, so sharing something as simple as a smile gains you happiness—a shared moment of internal joy!

Each of your engagements presents you with the opportunity to share various gifts of happiness with those around you. You can effortlessly change your environments by always wearing a smile on your face and by leaving laughter upon lips.

Thinking positive is not just about altering your thoughts. Positive thinking is inclusive of your actions, your deeds and your behaviors. You must *be* and also *do* positive within your life. If we can't first change your thoughts, you can always adjust your behaviors and *behave* things into existence.

Happiness and laughter first start with a smile.

Focus today on trailblazing with your smile!

Say Aloud: **I Will Smile! I Will Laugh! I Will Be Happy!**

I've got nothing to do today but smile.

PAUL SIMON

09 Kindness

"

I Will RESPECT Others!

"

Respect for another human being isn't *optional.*

Respect is REQUIRED!!!

Existence alongside others is just cause for you to esteem them as highly as you esteem yourself. You should regard yourself ***so*** highly that your respect for all others is readily apparent. In happiness, show your respect for others by way of admiration, honor and patience.

Affirmation Journal

★ **In what ways do I show respect for others?**

★ **In what ways am I lacking in showing respect for others?**

★ **What will it take for me to better respect others?**

Self-respect spills over into general respect for all mankind. Value yourself highly enough that your own esteem compels you to treat others with the utmost regard. If ever you become weary, stop in the moment and remind yourself that no one is worth you losing your self-respect over. Continually grow in love for yourself and bountifully apply the same to others.

Say Aloud: **I Will Respect Myself! I Will Respect Others!**

10 Kindness

“

I Will SERVE!

”

Service starts with humility. It's about honoring others with your assistance, your time and your resources. Service is about giving back while paying it forward. Your community deserves your services for all that it has taught you and allowed you to be. Acts of service demonstrate gratitude. What better way to show thanks than to help out?

This world deserves your services for all that it has been for you. Locally, you can join or create programs within your community that promote service, unity and betterment. Personally, you can mentor, volunteer and support those within your social environments. Professionally, you have the opportunity to participate in the efforts of your workforce to create friendly, profitable and knowledgeable work environments.

Affirmation Journal

★ **How do I serve?**

★ **How will I serve better/more in the future?**

★ **What does my act of service do for others?**

Say Aloud: **I Will Serve! I Will Give Back to Others!**

True humility is not thinking less of yourself;
it is thinking of yourself less.

C.S. LEWI

11

Kindness

"I Will Be USEFUL to Others!"

Having a fear of commitment is synonymous with having fear of SELF! Most people don't commit because they don't want to be counted on by others. They don't want to have anyone depending on their performance, which may not always be *great* at any given time. Instead of committing, they choose the lesser evil: being elusive and noncommittal. These fears are rarely, if EVER, about anyone other than *self*.

In order for YOU to be useful to others, remove the fears associated with commitment. There is no failure in commitment—there is only growth. Your life is fruitless if you don't share what you've been given. It's your job to plant seeds that grow into lifelong harvest for the benefit of all.

Being useful to others is as simple as using what we've been given.

What have YOU been given?

Affirmation Journal

★ **What do I have that is useful to others?**

★ **How do I give using what I have?**

★ **How does my usefulness help me in return?**

Say Aloud: **I Will Be Useful to Others! I Use What I Have!**

Kindness

"I Will Be a RESOURCE for Others!"

In all of your giving and serving and helping, you will find that the BEST thing you can EVER be to others is a resource. You don't have to be the person with ALL of the answers, but if people know that in you they have an invaluable treasure, they will want to connect with you both personally and professionally time and time again!

Resourcefulness is a timeless skill. By being proficient you not only service the needs of others, but you are well fit to obtain exactly what you need for *yourself*! Such adeptness takes you FAR in life as others will quickly see how shrewd you are based on your tenacious approach to EVERYTHING! You will be an inspiration who is well supported by all who are blessed to cross your path!

Affirmation Journal

★ **How resourceful am I?**

★ **How have others viewed me as a resource?**

★ **How do I use my resourcefulness to my own benefit?**

Say Aloud: I Will Be a Resource for Others!

A man of words and not of deeds
Is like a garden full of weeds.

ENGLISH PROVERB

13 Kindness

> "I LEAD!!!"

You are a leader! You are reading this book, so you already lead! **GREAT JOB!** Being the leader that you are, always be mindful to stay leadership-focused despite life. Don't ever allow life to get the upper hand in such a way that you fall from the good graces of your role as a leader! Followers follow because of the values consistent with leadership.

Pride yourself on always upholding values demonstrative of your inherent role as a leader. This doesn't mean you need to be superhuman! Show the REALITY of your humanity by being true to who you are and by leading first through example. The BEST leaders demonstrate resilience. While life is happening to everyone else, the example of the leader illustrates malleability—the ability to BOUNCE BACK!

Life doesn't quit—leaders don't either, so BE **CONSISTENT**! Be STRONG and courageous! Don't shake at every little sign of trouble. Be wise in your approach and methodical in your movements. Don't be hurried but make pointed progress with clear intent.

Say Aloud: **I Am Wise! I Take Action! I Am Consistent! I Lead!**

Journal Prompt...

Am I leading in life? ______ **How so?** ______________________

____

____

____

____

____

How can I make my role as a leader more apparent to myself and others?

____

____

____

____

____

14 Kindness

"

I TEACH!!!

"

You impart knowledge to others by teaching them the lessons that you've learned. The knowledge that you've acquired is shared with others to increase their own intelligence in any subject matter.

Words are typically thought of as the primary method used to teach *yet* there are a great many lessons taught using no words at all.

Understanding that teaching isn't limited to words, embrace teaching using various means. Recognize that others gain from you based on your lifestyle, your mistakes, your character and your decisions. People learn more from you based on these factors than they learn by simply hearing your words, so what are you teaching?

Affirmation Journal

★ **What are others learning through my example?**

★ **What are others learning through my words?**

★ **Are these messages similar OR are there mixed signals?**

Say Aloud: **I Teach! My Life is *the* Example of My Teaching!**

Preach the Gospel at all times,
and when necessary, use words.

Francis of Assisi

Kindness

"

I Am SHARING!

"

In charity and benevolence, show your favor toward others; in humility, provide gifts of time, talent and resources with the world around you; by way of your lifestyle, impart the growth that you've been blessed to experience. *This* is how you share.

Sharing is the pathway toward positivity in a world ripe with negativity! Sharing is great inspiration to all who receive its reward! Sharing is a means of support and encouragement, often unsolicited yet always available when needed.

You are purposed to share. Your life conditions you to be a recipient of sharing, so relish the opportunity to *return* the favor! When you share, you show that others have been MORE for you than you have sometimes been for yourself even in the smallest things.

Random and repeat acts of kindness show the epitome of the sharer's soul! Endeavor to touch MANY souls in the same manner that many have touched YOURS!

Say Aloud: **I Am Sharing! I Am *Showing* Kindness!**

Journal Prompt...

Do I allow kindness in my life? **What does that look like?**

Do I allow sharing in my life? **What does that look like?**

What are my kindness issues?

What are my sharing issues?

How can I resolve these issues?

Kindness

"

I DO!!!

"

What are you doing with your time? What are you doing with your life? What are you doing with all that you've been given? Are you taking actions that will change your life? Are you taking actions that will change your community?

Goals and dreams are nothing if you do nothing to achieve them. High regard and respect is nothing if you do nothing to show it. You must be a DOer! SHOW through your ACTIONS! If you take no action, what are you showing? What are you showing to *yourself* and what are you showing to others?

*Do*ers don't ask for permission—they take action! Instead of tip-toeing through your life looking for permission to take charge, COMMAND control by taking action to create the life you deserve! Be a *DO*ER!

Affirmation Journal

★ **What am I doing with my time?**

★ **What am I doing with my life?**

★ **What am I doing with all that I have been given?**

If you're not making mistakes,
then you're not doing anything.
I'm positive that a doer makes mistakes.

John Wooden

17 Kindness

"

I Will GIVE!

"

The MOST helpful people in life are those who are givers! Givers increase your potential by providing you with resources not otherwise at your disposal. They help you see that the world is even more beautiful than you once viewed it. Giving people cause you to be humble, grateful and... well, you learn to become a giver yourself!

Today's To-Do's...

★ **Give thanks to those who have helped you along the way.**

★ **List out people who have sown into you in the past.**

★ **For each of them, fulfill a random act of kindness.**

The act of giving solidifies the goal of kindness. Giving is a tangible means of showing kindness and supporting others. Humility results from awareness of the desire to move the passions of others forward as you simultaneously position *yourself* for forward mobility. Through giving, you also honor and thank those who have helped to pave the way for you in life.

Affirmation Journal

★ **Who have I supported through my giving?**

★ **How have my gifts benefited others?**

★ **How do my gifts benefit me?**

Say Aloud: **I Will Give! I Gift Others with My Support!**

Random Acts of Kindness

Use this listing to list 8 people you'd like to do something nice for.

8 People Who Have Sown into Me	
(Person Number 1's Name)	(Deadline)
(Person Number 2's Name)	(Deadline)
(Person Number 3's Name)	(Deadline)
(Person Number 4's Name)	(Deadline)
(Person Number 5's Name)	(Deadline)
(Person Number 6's Name)	(Deadline)
(Person Number 7's Name)	(Deadline)
(Person Number 8's Name)	(Deadline)

18 Kindness

" My Life is a GIFT! "

Life is a gift to be cherished and shared with those around you! The secrets of your life are unlocked with each opportunity you take to share more of yourself in deed and truth. You provide awakening for the souls of others when you expand yourself through giving. As you use our own gifts of light, you take the stand for others to do the same!

Embrace the gifts that God has given you. Embrace your LIFE! Understand that you are not here by mistake. Your life urges you to a higher calling through which you will fulfill your ultimate path. On the way toward that deeper meaning, challenge yourself to remove the bounds of fear so that you may expand beyond your wildest dreams!

Life is a gift!

What are you doing with yours?

Affirmation Journal

★ **How am I sharing the gift of my life with myself?**

★ **How am I sharing the gift of my life with others?**

★ **How am I sharing the gift of my life with God?**

Say Aloud: **My Life is a Gift!**

Do not be afraid; our fate
Cannot be taken from us; it is a gift.

DANTE ALIGHIERI

19 Kindness

“

I Am SUPPORTIVE!

”

Our society could stand to make GREAT gains in the area of support. Individually, each of us could stand to do the same!

Support is how you demonstrate advocacy for a particular person, product or platform. It's a way to honor and encourage gains made for the betterment of individual communities and of society as a whole. By being supportive, you not only endorse those with the courage to branch out, but you also increase awareness of steps necessary to back others who are doing the same.

Say Aloud: **I Am Supportive! I Will *Show* Support to Others!**

Always be willing to provide services and contributions to those who are setting the stage for change. This includes those within your immediate environment and also those with global scale. Support is shown in many ways and humble support isn't guided by personal gains for any contributions of time, effort or commitment, so don't support others based on whether they support you. Support your fellowman in the same manner that you would have him or her support you—in *true* humility and kindness.

Affirmation Journal

★ How supportive am I of others?

★ How supportive am I of myself?

★ In what ways will I show support in the future?

20 Kindness

"I Will Not Be a CRITIC!"

With all that you learn in life, these lessons are less about making firm assessments and more about learning how to best navigate within in a dynamic world.

All too often, many people voluntarily take the fruitless opportunity to place themselves within the role of critic. Insufficient details viewed from misinformed eyes are seemingly enough to make far-reaching judgments that consequently limit realization of objective viewpoints. These invalid critiques keep *everyone* from the goals of respect and diversity. Since it stifles interactions, poor judgment prevents diversity, unity, growth and creativity. People end up existing alone yet humans are inadequately equipped to traverse life alone.

Learn how to exist in this world without judging others. If you assess anyone at all, assess only yourself. Be your own governing authority where *facts* are the basis of your claims.

Say Aloud: **I Will Not Be a Critic! I Will Not Judge Others!**

The ability to observe without evaluating
is the highest form of intelligence.

JIDDU KRISHNAMURTI

21 Kindness

"I Will MENTOR!"

Mentoring presents you with the opportunity to give back to your respective community. Through mentoring you're able to pave the way for other bright individuals to access resources that may or may not have been shared with you. In seeing goodness in those around you, your hope should always be toward their betterment. Join top talent on their paths by offering them the advantage of mentorship whereby you instill values and skill-sets that will propel them into their BEST future! *You just can't pass up GREAT talent!*

Relish the opportunity to mentor a deserving individual! As much as they benefit from what is gained from *you*, you benefit all the more by what you gain from *them*!

After parenting, mentoring is the next BEST thing! ☺

It doesn't matter your race, age, occupation, religion, creed... **EVERYONE** is a prime candidate to mentor another individual! Informally, you already silently mentor based on your lifestyle, so take your stewardship to the next level and FORMALLY invite someone to be your mentee! Share with them the same knowledge you *wish* was shared with you!

Help another soul along on their journey throughout life!

Say Aloud: **I Will Mentor! I Will Pay It Forward!**

22 Kindness

"

I Will Speak LIFE!

"

Of all the words that escape your lips on any given day, how much of what you say is actually positive? How often can you count on yourself to verbalize affirming statements throughout the course of a single day? Think about it! Are you the Negative Nancy, Debbie Downer or Petty Patty of your group? Maybe you're a Melancholy Michael, Sickening Sam or Billy the Bully. If you are: **STOP!!!!**

NO ONE wants to be around you with all of your *constant* negativity!!! If you're honest with yourself, you realize that YOU don't even want to be around you! QUIT with all of the negative talk and be more positive in your life! Don't settle for just THINKING positive, but DO positive, BE positive and SPEAK positively! SAY ALOUD the things that you WILL achieve in life and stop always waiting around for someone else to encourage you or pat you on the back! DIY!

DO IT YOURSELF!!!!

In ALL that you *do* and in all that you *say* today, let it portray your path toward POSITIVISM! **SPEAK LIFE!!!**

Few things in the world are more powerful than a positive push.
A smile. A world of optimism and hope.
A 'you can do it' when things are tough.

RICHARD M. DEVOS

Journal Prompt...

How can I make a practice of speaking life into others on a daily basis?

23 Kindness

“

I Will SHARE!

”

Life is too short to disregard expressing thoughts of love, care, and concern. If there's someone that you love or someone that you miss, do what it takes to let them know!

All too often, people miss moments to show and to share in gratitude for others. Some people are *quick* to think that no one loves them and that no one cares.

BE the love that you want to receive! *Show* others the same acts of kindness, generosity and appreciation that you would want them to show you. Love and kindness toward others should never be about whether they will, or will not, show that same measure to you in return. Be kind *just because*! Be kind because it's the RIGHT thing to do and because random acts of kindness make you, the giver, feel just as good as the recipient!

Be random today!

SHARE!

Affirmation Journal

★ **When was the last time I shared my love for a friend?**

★ **How often do I share my appreciation for others?**

★ **Who, in my life, needs to know that I care about them?**

Say Aloud: **I Will Share! I Will Show Others Loving Kindness!**

24 Kindness

"I Will Spread GOOD CONTAGION!"

During speaking engagements, I explain to participants that I SPEAK with **exclamation points**!!! I even use considerable exclamation points within my written communication! Exclamation points are a tenant of my personality! The more exclamation points I *use*, the more exclamation points I *feel*!

Imagine how people perceive you, and your life, when you use exclamation points. Of course, you can't bank *wholly* on perception here, but OH THE **JOY** when *perception* of exclamation points becomes *reality* for you! Ohhhhh… You have LIVED at that point!

The world (i.e. **LIFE!**) could present you with trial upon trial, yet trials are only trials if you *view* them as such. Think about it! The goal, then, is to change your way of *thinking*. The more you *view* life as positive, the more positive life will BE!

Bring JOY to your life and also to the lives of others. A person always has good things to say about those who helped them laugh, smile and LIVE! Spread good contagion!

I do believe we're all connected.
I do believe in positive energy.
I do believe in the power of prayer.
I do believe in putting good out into the world.
And I believe in taking care of each other.

HARVEY FIERSTEIN

Journal Prompt...

What does the following quote mean to me? *I Will Spread Good Contagion!*

25 Kindness

"

I SHOW!

"

Kindness is the practice of doing unto others as you would have them do unto you. It involves practices of sacrifice, humility and peace, in love. The best role that you can take in kindness is that of the leader, the giver, the *doer*. *Show* kindness to others and kindness will be received back to you! Believe the best of others and let your leadership show them how to do the same. Be the BEST example you can be in showing character that is resilient, refined and REMARKABLE. Without being haughty, give others a reason to *be* and to *do* better for themselves by seeing *your* fine example.

Say Aloud: **I Am a Leader! I Am a Giver! I Am a Doer! I *Show*!**

In your demonstrations of kindness, be a model of diplomacy. Let your humility speak VOLUMES by how you show random acts of kindness as much as you possibly can. Without having an expectation of ANYTHING, show others the same amount of kindness, generosity and love as you would like to receive from them in return.

Affirmation Journal

★ How can I show that I believe the best of myself?

★ How can I show that I believe the best of others?

★ **How can I show that I am a model of leadership?**

Kindness

"

I Am a VESSEL!

"

Don't be under the impression that your life exits only for you—it doesn't. Don't think that every lesson that you learn is only for you—it isn't. Don't think that you are here only to help yourself—you aren't! Get it? Got it?! GOOD!

Life is SO much bigger than who you are and what you can accomplish by your own right. Life is composed of self PLUS every little thing, big thing, seen and unseen, real or fake thing that comes within your awareness—that includes people. Don't make the mistake of living as if the things you experience exist only for your own personal growth. Some of what you experience happens for everyone else BUT you! Ever consider that?! You've existed in someone's life at some point simply because of what *you* had to offer *them*! The experience existed for you *solely* because of what you were in the moment for another human being. Let that simmer.

Life exists for you to guide yourself. It also exists for you to guide others to be better. Be the vessel that you were created to be. Be all things to all people. Teach and let them learn.

Say Aloud: **I Am a Vessel! My Life Exists for Others Too!**

My religion is very simple.
My religion is kindness.

Dalai Lama XIV

27

Kindness

"

I SHARE!

"

Sharing is Caring!

It's true! Sharing *is* caring. The contributions that you invest into others are a telltale sign of your care and concern for them. Sharing isn't limited to direct gifts of time, money or other physical means of giving—you share through your lifestyle, your character and through expressions of goodness shown within your interactions.

In being resourceful, share the information you have at your disposal and give others the knowledge that you've received. In being gifted in various skill-sets, share your gifts as a volunteer, teacher or business owner while giving back your talents as goods or services. In being committed to acts of kindness, share through mentoring, helping and bettering *yourself* so that you may give back to your community the value that was once given to you.

Commit to sharing *all* that you have to give. Don't limit your engagement with life by not sharing who you are with the ENTIRE world! Deeper meaning and solid connections are found when you share. Sharing opens the door for growth, both internally and outwardly into the world.

What will YOU share?

Affirmation Journal

★ **What additional growth could be seen within my world if I learned to share more?**

28

Kindness

"I Will Serve My COMMUNITY Better!"

Community service makes the world go 'round! Without serving your immediate community *first*, you truly miss the **ULTIMATE MISSION** of individualistic service to all humanity. Service and community go hand in hand. They act right alongside unity, pride and resolution. Of all that ails the world, humanity would find FERVENT resolve should people venture to place their efforts *directly* into the communities where they reside. Anytime you look around your own environment and think,"Something's missing!", *that* is the exact moment that you should follow up with an action-prone brainstorm targeted to fix whatever is broken—provide whatever is missing. You can't be disappointed by what you don't endeavor to change.

The feeling of disappointment is a **Call to ACTION**:

DO Something About It!!!

Complaints are impractical when you can *always* be a FACILITATOR of change.

Instead of simply *talking*, start serving!

Say Aloud: **I Will Serve My Community Better!!!**

The best index to a person's character is how he treats people who can't do him any good, and how he treats people who can't fight back.

Abigail Van Buren

29 Kindness

"

I WILL GO GREEN!

"

Socially, responsibilities are boundless. You have a duty to serve your community through efforts that will change society, and in turn, impact the world.

What are YOU doing to impact lasting change within your environment?

The Go Green cause has been developed to prolong use of resources within the environment. Practices have been implemented that will extend the lifespan of natural resources so that they may be useful to future generations. Help these initiatives by recycling goods that are able to be reused. Re-purpose items and make a commitment to be more mindful when using resources. By increasing awareness on the topic, you learn that there are a great many ways to Go Green in practice.

Going Green starts with a mindset to lead a less wasteful life. As you become more socially responsible and supportive toward just causes, you also challenge others to do the same.

How are YOU going green?

Say Aloud: **I Will Go Green! I Challenge *Others* to Go Green!**

Journal Prompt...

In what ways will I Go Green?

1. ____________________________________
2. ____________________________________
3. ____________________________________
4. ____________________________________
5. ____________________________________

Why is this important?

____

____

____

30

Kindness

“

I Will Be KIND!

”

As a child, one of the first skills that you are taught is kindness. You learn how to share and how to be aware of your playmates with the hope of developing into an adult who readily embraces fellowship and friendship.

Kindness, in all of its golden simplicity, is the easiest—yet sometimes most difficult—of all traits. Kindness is all too often based on your mood in any given moment which means your ability to *fulfill* acts of kindness flexes numerous times within any given day. Exhibitions of kindness shouldn't rest so heavily on your moods. If you are to change your moods to be more positive, acts of kindness are a GREAT place to start! By showing others positivity, you reap the same happiness that you graciously sow.

Don't ever let a sour mood detour you from doing something kind for another. No matter what is done to you, share love by being kind to everyone you come in contact with. The rewards of your good nature will be evidenced by your pure heart, your gentle spirit and by the lasting calm that will encircle your life. Let your kindness speak for you!

Be nice.
And if you can't do that, just don't be mean.

Richelle E. Goodrich

Journal Prompt...

I Will Be KIND because ____

____

____

____

____

____

____

____

____

31 Kindness

"

"

Write Your Kindness Affirmation Thoughts Here!

Write Your Own Kindness Quote Here!

Your Picture Here!

but wait!

There's More!

Additional reader-only content including worksheets, workbooks, writing prompts and journals can be found at www.Change-Your-Posture.com. Visit us for resources on this book and others within the Change Your Posture series.

I would LOVE to personally connect with you!

Attn: Coach D Nicole!
Sh'Shares NETWORK
1601-1 N Main St 13202
Jacksonville, FL 32206

www.Change-Your-Posture.com
www.CoachDNicole.com
www.ShShares.com

Send book praise and reading group pictures to:

SHINE@Change-Your-Posture.com

It is my sincere prayer that you were blessed by the contents of this book. I look forward to securing our connection well into the future!

Thank you for your GREATNESS!

Coach D Nicole is a very charming and spirited first-class professional who is passionate about encouraging, supporting and coaching others within their personal lives and business endeavors. As a transformational life coach, she is most loved for her wit, boisterous personality, direct and upfront coaching style, and generous, authentic smile!

www.ingramcontent.com/pod-product-compliance
Ingram Content Group UK Ltd.
Pitfield, Milton Keynes, MK11 3LW, UK
UKHW062001290726
14090UKWH00021B/1328

9 781942 650379